'AN ARTIST AMONG THE ASHES'

A photographic record at the very end of Southern Region steam

DAVID SHEPHERD

Noodle Books

ISBN 978-1-906419-67-7

First published in 2012 by Kevin Robertson under the **NOODLE BOOKS** imprint
PO Box 279, Corhampton, SOUTHAMPTON. SO32 3ZX

www.noodlebooks.co.uk

Printed in England by Ian Allan Printing.

David sketching at Ryde, O2's 'Merstone' and 'Fisbourne' in the last days of British Rail. This is where the dream of owning my own steam engine began, but that's another story.

Introduction

It was early in 1967 that I realised that steam was going and going very fast, to the scrapyards. For my part, I was therefore painting in my studio all day and then, at every opportunity, collecting up my oil paints and camera and dashing off to the nearest steam shed, Guildford and other sheds to record something of the emotional last months. In some cases, I only managed a few brush strokes before the locomotive was towed away.

When negotiations started for the preparation of this book I was astonished to find that I had taken such a vast number of photographs. They had been tucked away in a cupboard and I found an enormous box of transparencies which I had forgotten all about. When I was gathering all this material, I had no intention of it being seen. All the photographs and sketches were simply providing me with invaluable material to be used in creating major works such as Black Five Country to be painted in the comfort of my studio. When working in the steam sheds, I was not interested in accuracy and detail. It was simply a question of trying to record atmosphere through my camera lens and my pallet. Atmosphere to me meant little nuances such as the gorgeous colour of a pool of oil on the floor catching the sunlight. I was fascinated by shafts of sunlight coming through a shed roof encrusted with soot, firing irons hanging on a hook, an old steam crane such as that at Fratton, all adding up to a scene of degradation but with an atmosphere tinged with sadness.

Now, in my 80th year, I have seen some sense in releasing whatever my camera and canvas have portrayed, hoping that it will rekindle memories of those sad days, now so long ago. Many people have asked why I always paint such sad railway paintings. It is simply because I believe that a locomotive covered in grime with sad messages chalked on the smoke box, "Farewell old friend", mean so much more than a clean locomotive, of which there were very few in those days at the end of steam.

David Shepherd

Cover - *The products of Messrs. Riddles and Bulleid face each other amongst the grime of Nine Elms.*

Frontispiece - *No. 80012.*

Right - *Tea in hand: seen from the canteen at Guildford.*

The Stage at Nine Elms

One of the most exciting features of Nine Elms was the giant coaling stage. Here there was drama indeed; over years of neglect, the crack under the stage had sunk some considerable amount. This meant that the Bulleid pacifics would gently come down and stop, to be coaled. Then, all hell was let loose. After four or five attempts, with wheels screaming, the locomotive managed to escape her torture, inch by inch to carry on her journey to Waterloo.

Right - There will be no more coaling for this Standard 4-6-0.

People often ask me why I always paint sad locomotive pictures. The answer is a simple one, a dirty engine covered in grime and filth through neglect, can tell far more stories than a clean engine straight out of works.

One of the most exciting features of Nine Elms was the giant coaling stage. Here there was drama indeed; over years of neglect, the crack under the stage had sunk some considerable amount. This meant that the Bulleid pacifics would gently come down and stop, to be coaled. Then, all hell was let loose. After four or five attempts, with wheels screaming, the locomotive managed to escape her torture, inch by inch to carry on her journey to Waterloo.

Left - Inside the cathedral like interior of Nine Elms. What stories might be told of past times.

Right - No. 34047 (withdrawn 25 June 1967), dead and surplus to requirements. In the haste of withdrawal the numberplate and rods have been removed but there is still a 'white' headcode disc displayed - it will not be going anywhere else apart from to the scrap merchants.

35013

Walking through a diesel shed can make me feel sick.
A steam shed – no way, just dirt and soot and smoke.
Interestingly the whole area around this part of London in
1967displayed an air of dereliction; the great masterpiece of
Battersea Power Station in the distance in a shameful state of
disrepair, just like the locomotives in the shed.

Despite the attempt by nature to re-colonise the area with
green it is doubtful if the area beyond the engines was little
more than weed. Indeed what natural fauna could survive in
this expanse of ash?

Seen from the coaling stage the signal box over the main line
casts a watchful gaze, its days too would be numbered.

The tank engines were the last of the breed, their role to move
carriages in and out of Waterloo - as well as giving departing
trains a 'shove' as far as the end of the platform. Such niceties
would be irrelevant to 'electric multiple units'.

Above - Exciting colours, oil, muck and sunlight.

Right - Sunlight could change perspective in so many ways,
dust particles dancing in the sun, the glimpse of purple seen
across the spectrum of light, and here to the engine head
lamp -viewed against the light it takes on a different
dimension.

Left - I clambered on top of a Bulleid pacific to do this sketch. Painted from life, the 'blue colour' is the evening sky reflected in a puddle of rain water on the roof of the driver's cab.

Right - There were many opportunities to get seriously hurt walking around in the semi darkness and tripping on pieces of locomotive, in this case the end cover from the piston valve and part of the front framing left on the floor.

Once a proud member of the 'Merchant Navy' class. Now an inconspicuous member of the class shorn of any name identification.

With only a few weeks to go, there were often more railway enthusiasts in the shed than staff and, inevitably, there was quite a lot of pilfering, to which a blind eye was usually turned. People genuinely wanted mementoes of their favourite locomotive. In this case, the number from the front of the locomotive has been stolen and the only form of identification was a rough quick chalk mark. Good looking coal on the right but with some ready to fall off soon after moving. To the residents of the nearby flats the end of steam could not come soon enough as within minutes of hanging their washing out it would be covered in soot. . What was once acceptable was now criticised - as were the enthusiasts who attempted to gain access to balconies for that 'one-off' high-level photograph. Often at Nine Elms in 1967, when I was sketching, it seems that there were more railway enthusiasts in the shed and yard than there were railway staff; jumping across inspection pits and climbing on the locomotives, through all this BR were still trying to run a railway!

Above - One of my most memorable moments. Here we see 35030, "Elder Dempster Line" which had received a bit of attention from the cleaners. The moment I cherish the memory of is, when walking past the grime encrusted locomotive, I just had the urge to remove some of this filth to see what was underneath. Sure enough, rubbing her with my handkerchief exposed a sudden explosion of colour came through the dirt – beautiful Brunswick green with the orange and black lining which was the livery in the days of British Rail.

Right - The Bulleid with the longest name 'Sir Eustace Missenden - Southern Railway', honouring the last Chairman of the Southern who went on to become the first Chairman of British Railways. The scaffolding seems more to do with propping up the shed roof than the engine. Minor 'signs of conflict' in the form of the bend front footstep. No. 34090 would survive until the very end having run an average of just over 40,000 a year since new in 1949.

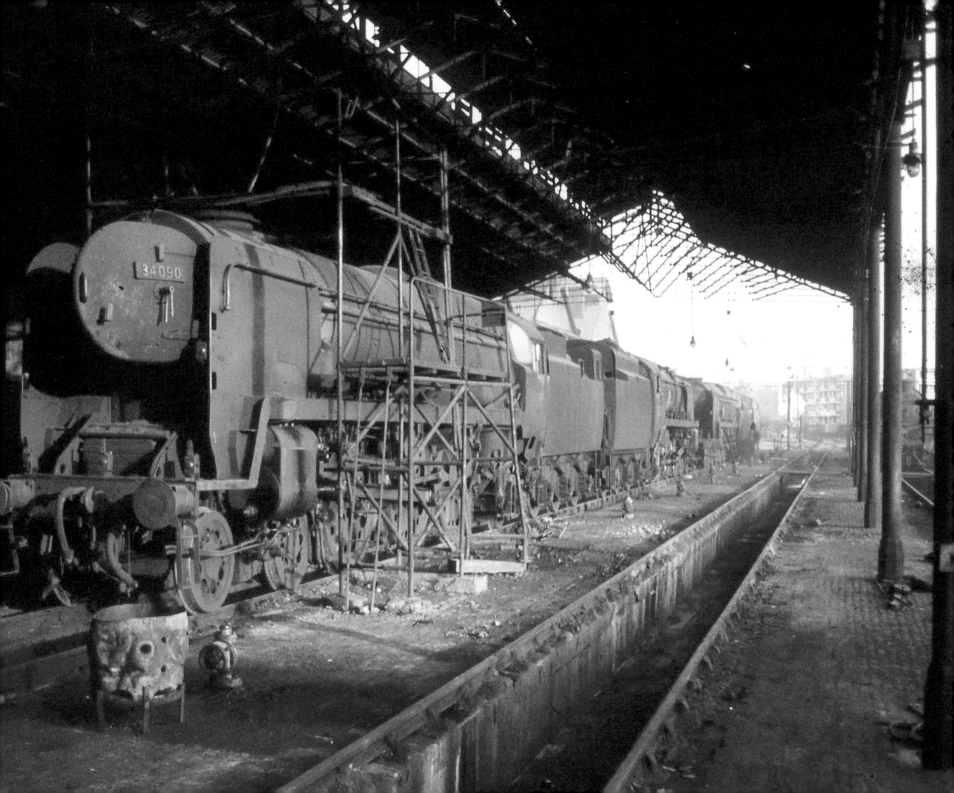

Today's obsession with Health & Safety would have a fit. Limited footing, no safety rails, and a drop of 10-12 feet made worse by various solid obstructions en-route - and that is to say nothing of the ash itself. This was one of just two original Bulleid types which lasted until the end, possible No. 34023.

Piles of ash are witness to the countless engines that had to be serviced at this point. Once any such accumulation of rubbish would have been cleared away almost straight away – hence the empty wagons into which the char would eventually be deposited. Towards the end of steam, it was just allowed to accumulate everywhere. It was heart breaking as I knew only too well the dedication and indeed love that loco men, drivers and fitters showed towards the engines. Now, everything was derelict; there was no incentive whatsoever to keep the place reasonably presentable. It was not surprising that British Rail had so much trouble recruiting staff to work under such conditions for less pay than could be achieved elsewhere. Such was the amount of emotion generated by the scene at Nine Elms that some of the engine men actually raised enough money to save their engine, 'Blackmoor Vale'. I wonder if this locomotive is actually her before having a bath? I couldn't possibly tell under the grime.

In the foreground are the stumps of the original coaling stage, redundant and forgotten. Its successor soon to follow a similar fate.

During daylight hours large white indicator discs would inform railway staff the destination of the train. At night the electric lights might have been used although tradition dies hard and an oil lamp remained a regular feature. The case of the oil lamp should be white, that of the electric lamps polished brass.

Above - Rust forms quickly on non moving parts although in this case this Standard at least will breath another day.

Opposite page, bootm left - Masses of lovely colour here with flashes of colour; hot oil dripping down the rods and wisps of steam. The effect of water on oil and the yellow foam that results. The basic drip lubrication of the steam engine meant that oil would be flung in all directions when moving, hence the built up of dirt and dust itself attracted to the resultant goo. Hard to imagine that decades before a driver would wipe a clean white handkerchief along similar parts and woo-betide the cleaner responsible if there a trace of dirt collected.

Top right - Early 1967, No 35014 above, still in service, just, yet some years older than the withdrawn tank engine alongside.

Bottom right - I as getting very excited while I was painting this sketch but they towed the engine away in front of me.

Engines with potentially years of useful life left in them were cast aside the moment anything other than a straightforward repair was needed. Sometimes stripped of parts to keep others of like type working, other times, such as here, the rods removed from this Standard tank and just left on the ground. Death occurring where they had last breathed steam, not even the dignity of being pulled to one side out of view. The men (railway employees or visitors?) are likely discussing that very same waste of resource.

Right - Comparisons inside Nine Elms, One "Blackmoor Vale" had been saved for preservation, hence its clean condition. The other "Salisbury", one of the last Bulleids to be in service at the end, its filthy condition lit by one of the lights of the shed, was hauled away for scrap a week later.

Right - Another engine receiving care and attention, No 35028, selected for private preservation, at the time considered to be the only one likely to survive.

Left - A rebuilt Merchant Navy, impressive and in the minds of many, aesthetically one of the best looking of any steam engine of later years.

Above - Nos. 34034 and 75075, no longer required for service. On the extreme right a brighter future awaits No 41298 which has been secured for preservation initially at Longmoor and then at Quainton in 1970, where work began on what was a long term overhaul.

Left - Although replenished, the tender of No 34093 does not seem to contain much in the way of quality coal whilst a fair proportion of perhaps better fuel lies scattered on the ground. Smart green paint reposes under the layers of grime, but aesthetically others were far worse. It would not take much to restore some sense of pride.

Above - The curved side tanks immediately indicate this was an engine designed at Brighton. Notwithstanding being of the Standard type, in profile the curvature matched the Southern Bulleid coaches - accident or design?

Above - Customary headgear on a steam engine - the knotted handkerchief, preferred by some as more practical than the issue cap, to others it was seen as more attractive to female passengers…….

Right - Inside the shed illumination was by daylight or a few electric bulbs swinging high in the roof. The trolley might be used for oil cans and the like but as with the steam engines has clearly seen better days.

No doubt cleaned by volunteers rather than railway staff, No 34052 formerly carried the name 'Lord Dowding'. Despite the smarter appearance than its neighbours, such niceties would not help at the end and as with its neighbours it would be cut up and recycled; a journey to the scrapyard followed by the steel shipped to Japan - retuning as part of a Japanese car perhaps?

Nos. 34077 above and 34071 right. The latter having already lost its squadron badge - illicitly perhaps. Neither would survive to the very end being withdrawn in the spring of 1967.

If shed scenes had been left just as they were at the end of steam, these places would now be massive tourist attractions.

The sale of the land at Nine Elms resulted in the new Covent Garden market. Guildford is now the inevitable multi-storey car park.

Morning steaming, the same sight as would be taking place at Guildford, Eastleigh, Salisbury, Bournemouth Weymouth etc. - as well as at the surviving sheds on the Midland and North Eastern regions.

This was a time rarely seen by the enthusiasts, they would arrive later, for the present the railwaymen have the depot to themselves. Men arriving for work, part way through a shift, and even going home. Some would have had an easier time than others, perhaps the delays last night had been few, perhaps the engine and coal had been in good order.

'An Artist Amongst the Ashes'. Canvas and easel within the confines of the shed.

What a panorama faced me when entering the shed for this particular photograph; I felt I was walking into a great cathedral.

It was not just the sights either, there were the sounds, steam escaping, the groan of wheels upon rails - the associated vibration as tons of metal came ever closer - and the creaking, as boilers and fireboxes expanded or contracted when heating up or cooling.

Whilst sight and sound might be recorded, what was not possible to retain was the smell. A mixture hard to describe to those who have not witnessed it, but a mixture, of smoke, steam, hot oil, and in places decay and damp.

Like separate oasis, one would move from gloom into light, from warmth into cold. With the engines around it was alive, but in places there was an air of decay and with each visit that pervading sense seemed to grow ever stronger.

Left - Whether it is an English beechwood, a scene of elephants in Africa, or Nine Elms, nature creates the most fantastic colours in the evening.

Above - If only we could capture the sound from the photograph, with drain cocks blasting steam, 34032 backs out of the shed for what will be, probably, one of her last journeys.

Left - The dramatic transformation when light enters. Against the dirt is a sign of something bright and fresh to come.

Right - In contrast, under the coaling stage. I doubt if much track maintenance was ever carried out in this are - how could it - with hungry engines queuing at all hours. The twisted railings and torn fittings tell their own story. Every one a memory, now lost forever.

Right - Dirt, debris and firing irons, lovely material for an artist, but tragic.

Quenching the thirst whilst, left, the engine crew may be glimpsed doing the same. Steam may have appeared glamorous from the platform and lineside, but in reality it was dirty, hard manual labour. The various supposed labour-saving devices introduced over the years doing little to improve the working conditions for footmen staff and fitters. Indeed some might even have been said to have had the opposite effect.

During those last dramatic months of early 1967 when steam began to disappear in the South of England with increasing speed, the drivers and fitters tried to give their locomotives some degree of dignity so parts such as the hinges on the smoke box door would be painted white. But when the days finally came in July 1967, even the white highlights started to fade.

.

Once upon a time the withdrawal or transfer of steam engines away from a depot would mean replacement machines would arrive, sometimes to a newer design, other times to concentrate a particular type in one place or even to deal with a seasonal increase in workings.

So the fires were lit, almost for the last time. The steam raiser doing his rounds by day and night with kindling, waste, and matches. Having checked the boiler was well filled with water he would next ensure the valves were set in mid gear, the regulator closed and hand-brake applied.

Now would come the time to breath life into the machine. Arranging his wares in the correct order, the fire was lit and a few carefully chosen lumps of coal added. Then the firebox doors would be closed, it was time to wait.

He would return several times over the next few hours to tend the fire, the results of his work manifest by the smoke coursing from the chimney and, after a few hours, the water starting to pulse in the gauge glass. The next visible sign was the needle of the pressure gauge beginning to move although it would be some hours before there was sufficient pent up energy to enable movement to take place.

Before this he would have handed over to the designated crew who would finish off the preparation and who had arrived perhaps one hour before the engine was due to leave the shed.

Such was the labour intensity of steam. The bigger the engine the longer the preparation time.

Even so their work was not finished as they worked the train. The engine would be checked at intervals along the route, oiled again, plus more water and sometimes coal, taken.

Comparison perhaps, although not very well, with the motor cars of the period. Reliable over a short distance only and requiring the carrying of numerous spanners and spares.

Modern traction is like the modern motor car. Fuel it and forget it - for a while at least. This had been aim of men like Bulleid, a steam engine intended to be worked for long periods and requiring little attention in-between times. Sadly the results were perhaps not as might have been wished, but no one should be blamed for trying.

Right - A rare sight indeed at the end; a merchant navy, 35008 was still sporting her name plate, which by now was taking on an enormous value as a reminder of the days of steam. Indeed, the name plate, if or when auctioned, probably would have gone for a higher sum than that achieved from cutting the engine up.

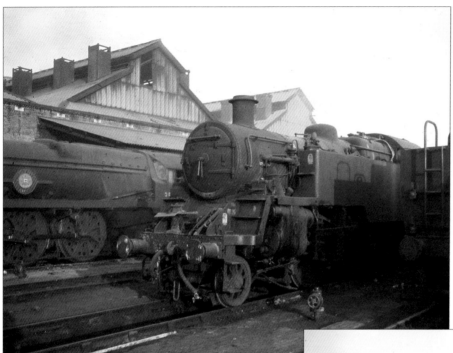

'Merchant Navy' class engines - and a forlorn 82xxx series tank engine.

In the top view No. 35012 'United States Line' in BG 'grime' livery keeps station with a former Waterloo pilot / shunting engine, its days now done.

A few years earlier No. 35012 had been polished to perfection for special train duty in connection with the presentation of LNER 'A4' 'Dwight D Eisenhower' to the American National Railroad Museum at Green Bay, Wisconsin.

At the time it was though No. 35012 might follow suit but that was not to be. Withdrawn due to a bad steam blow past the regulator valve it was unceremoniously dumped at Nine Elms and later towed away for scrap.

By comparison, sister engine, No 35028 survived, although this was not the first choice for preservation, that had been No 35022.

During the last days of steam all over the country a vast number of enthusiasts were dedicated to try and save as many locomotives as possible. Through the effort of so many of us, a large number were saved and Clan Line, seen here clean at Nine Elms is still with us some 40 years later.

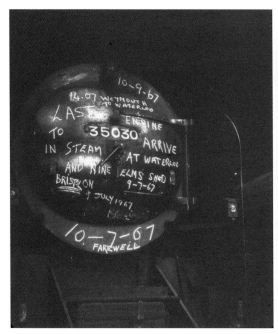

The last few weeks in the south of England was a highly emotional time when, on arrival at the scrapyards, the locomotives were covered in farewell messages; Merchant Navy Pacific 35030 was in fact the last locomotive to haul a scheduled service into Waterloo Station on Sunday 9 July 1967. After this she ran to Nine Elms for the fire to be dropped. She was still there, but now lifeless on Sunday 22 July.

.

But time marches on and those who at he time rued the introduction of diesel and electric traction would display similar nostalgia when the products of 1967 were themselves consigned to history.

By early 1968, the scrap merchants and contractors have won the day. There is no longer a locomotive shed at Nine Elms.

Last Hours at Nine Elms

This print was published to portray the last steam locomotive to enter Waterloo hauling a service train on
Sunday 9 July 1967; she would then steam into the shed, the fire would be dropped and the locomotive died.
This print sold in many thousands; the original painting was lost with five other major railway paintings in a fire.

The turntable at Guildford was vacuum operated with the comings and goings of the shed easily visible from the end of platform. Generations of young boys had stood at the south end of the station watching, nowadays there is nothing to look at.

Space was always cramped at Guildford, hence ashes would sometimes even be raked out inside the shed - the dust was terrible. That explains the presence of the wagon which would have arrived via the turntable. Painted from life just days before the shed closed, this scene was exactly the sort of subject I was always looking for; much more than a clean engine, the subtle colours of a locomotive half in sunlight and half in shadow.

WITHDRAWN — TWO MONTHS TO GO — MAY 1967

In this sketch, Bere Alston had just come in for an intermediate overhaul and I overheard one of the fitters saying "Don't do a decent job mate, she'll be scrapped anyway". What a shock to their morale after years of taking pride in their work.

Themes around the last Standards at Guildford,
both in service and withdrawn.

Bottom right - This is perhaps one of my more successful
sketches as there was no panic that the engine might be
towed away at any minute. The white strip is in fact sunlight
catching the edge of the inspection pit, giving the painting an
extra interest in amongst all the smoke.

Left - A feature of Guildford shed, well know to countless enthusiast was the fact that the engine man's cabin was situated right against the chalk face.

Right - As at Nine Elms, the building would come alive when an engine was about to move.

Engines under repair. These sheds had spare capacity to patch things up for just a little longer. This is a valve examination of No. 34034.

More Bulleid types, No. 34018 and one other, in disguise as its front number-plate and name have been removed.

Only a few years earlier engines such as these would have been reserved for the for the main line express workings, now what steam duties remained were handled by whatever was left, what was serviceable and available.

GUILDFORD SHED - FROM OFF - 10.30p - 4.30am

David Shepherd

Above - This painting is the only one I have lost a whole night's sleep over. A night scene in Guildford Shed, I started the painting at 10 pm and finished it at 4.30 am. The effort was worth every second. Paying no attention to detail, because that didn't matter, it was simply the steam and smoke and colours created by engines just about to go to the scrapyard, working on the canvas with just the dim light of one soot-encrusted light bulb above my head. I made no attempt at technical accuracy – a camera would provide that. The conditions were terrible, painting with only the aid of one soot-encrusted light bulb but I hope I managed to achieve some of the atmosphere, now lost forever.

Opposite page - Coming in off the turntable. The oil lamps of limited use.

Perhaps slightly cleaner than at Nine Elms - but only just.

Smoke and steam in the rafters. I wanted to capture the silhouette of the steam engine - the type was of less consequence - additionally, when I saw things that depicted the everyday working life - the screwed up newspaper on the driver's seat - this I came across quite by accident.

Painting in Guildford Shed.

Above - A live engine is facing a dead one. There was simply no room to store withdrawn engines so they were left wherever there was a space. The coaling stage for Guildford shed is on the right.

Right - A wipe of the rag was necessary to achieve some form of identification, '87' translates to '73087'. The firing iron adds an extra touch of interest for a painting.

B.R. Class 5
in filthy condition

in sunlight — under GUILDFORD coaling stage
hence v. dark background

note rust marks on boiler —

Studies in a withdrawn 'Class 5', less than 20 years old and with years of po
tial life ahead of her. Previous occasions of excess heat have burned off so
the paint, allowing rust to form; this gives my sketch an added dimension. T
sketch is of the locomotive in sunlight, standing against the interior of the co
shed.

As at Nine Elms, at the end of steam, there was no attempt to keep the shed and its surroundings clean and tidy. Engines were stripped wherever they stood, someone else could pick up the pieces.

Towards the end it was Standard types from the 1950s that dominated the scene. Even so the antiquated method of coaling remained - a metal stillage placed against the door of a wagon the door opened and coal would cascade into it. That was the easy bit, then the spills would be picked up whilst as the wagon contents diminished so more shovelling was required. The full stillage was then lifted up above the tender ready to be emptied.

Sunday 9 July 1967. The last engines have gone and for the first time in more than a century, all is quiet. The shed was soon to be knocked down to be replaced with the inevitable car park, but the memories are still there.

FRATTON AND A FINAL TRIP WITH STEAM

Left - I am so pleased to have recorded her in this photograph as she was the locomotive on which I had many illegal footplate rides which seemed to be going nowhere in particular. They were usually ballast trains, taking ballast from Guildford to heaven knows where. On many occasions we were called into a siding to allow a service train to pass and the result was endless cups of tea with the driver and fireman, talking about the great days of steam soon to finish altogether for them and the locomotives.

Below - Fratton; until steam came on the scene, I had never even heard of the place. I photographed from the cab this particular journey, arriving at possibly Redhill. Here, I also photographed an interloper. No. 77014 was not meant to be on the Southern Region but somehow had arrived from elsewhere, intending to only stay a short time before being returned to her territory, I believe north of the Thames. Instead, the locomotive was kept and formed a useful addition to a dwindling fleet of locomotives on Fratton shed. In this particular photograph, she is standing on what is now a housing estate.

As Fratton, as with Guildford, the end saw the steam fleet almost entirely dominated by standard types, a clean No. 73065 behind a smaller No. 76067. Possibly No. 73965 had been used for a recent special working. Behind the hated diesel - years later some loathing had been forgotten and they too achieved a considerable following.

Above - Hard to imagine this was the almost the end of steam, nothing but steam to be seen! Very rarely does any scene offer a perfect composition for an artist, but this fits the bill and is one of my very favourite pictures of all time.

Right - Of all the vast number of photographs that I took in those crazy weeks, this particular shot gives me almost more satisfaction than any other. Forget the details and the numbers of the engines; interesting little features such as the platform steps and the coal bucket – all super material. The defunct water column was there too and a much younger David Shepherd about to hop up onto the cab of 75074 for a cup of tea. Len Boxall leans out of the cab.

This shows the coaling stage at Fratton. It too would soon be redundant and scrapped.

She is so filthy that it is nearly impossible to even see the number on the cab side.

Permanent way train to Shalford? The original number plate had disappeared somewhere but to give the locomotive some dignity, the fitters in Guildford shed knocked a new plate up and I still have it as a wonderful memento.

Forlorn Fratton, similar to Guildford but a full roundhouse. However a roundhouse without a roof, in part, never fully replaced after bomb damage in WW2.

Here once engines from both the former LBSCR and LSWR had been serviced, more recently it had been the repository for several withdrawn steam engines considered for preservation. Some would be saved, others that should been, were not. Just the ghosts of men and machines remain.

Winter 1967/68 at Salisbury.

Salisbury winter 1967/68. A brazier to keep the last remaining men warm - once upon a time it would have been a cosy footplate. At first glace they have arrived from and are ready for duty, but look more closely and the rods have been removed. The only move that will come now is a tow to the scrapyard.

No. 34060 stripped and quietly rusticating. Look closely near the cylinder and timber packing is in place making it easier to be towed down to the scrapyard.. The tender also emptied of water and coal, neither the water column nor coaling stage will be needed again. In close up (right) the brake lever is seen through the open window.

Left - No cleaners to wipe away the grime although No. 30064 at least arrived in proud condition.

Right - No. 80016 alongside piles of discarded buckets and other items. Look carefully where the connecting rods have been stacked up on top of the tank.

Far right - A mixture of oil, a build up of rubbish and sunlight altogether creating the most glorious combination of colours – exciting for an artist!

Old fashioned coaling stage, and modern (then) coach livery.

Engines arrived and waiting to be dealt with, coal will be one of the first items to be removed. As at Fratton, the bag has disappeared from the water column.

Conversation time perhaps between engines, recalling perhaps the trains they once hauled, or deluding themselves that rescue and a return to service will come.

Another one stripped and tied, ready to move. A modern day notice cautions against overhead live wires.

A once proud Merchant Navy Pacific, not just 120 tons of scrap, mainly steel to the value at the time of perhaps £2,500; I think we paid less than that for Clan Line! The nameplate 'Orient Line - Merchant Navy Class' has already gone. Years later the price for just one of these pieces of brass (there were two, one on each side) would be perhaps ten times the scrap value of the complete engine.

Dear old 73155 once again, awaiting her fate.

As they arrived so certain parts were removed before being shunted on to a storage road, from here they would be removed a few at a time and towed to South Wales.

Just 20 years old, a USA type, once used in Southampton Docks, again with rods heaved up out of the way.

Slowly rusting, look carefully to see the missing parts.

Even months or years of grease will eventually succumb to the elements, to be replaced by dry rust.

Overleaf - Our proud and great steam age should have gone out in a blaze of glory. This was another blaze, utterly shameful and very sad.